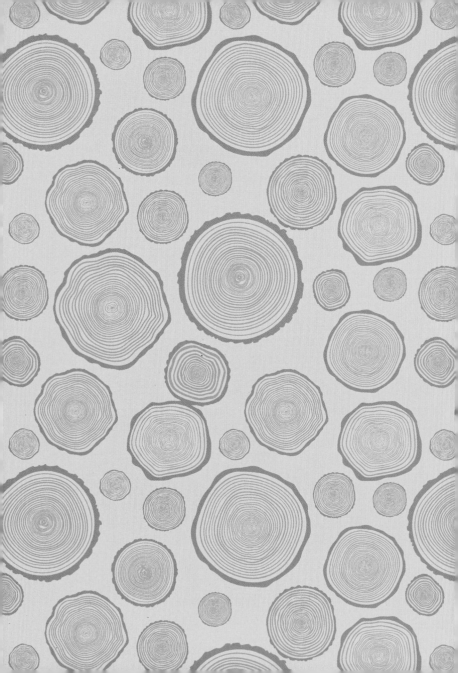

FIRE

THE COMPLETE GUIDE
FOR HOME, HEARTH, CAMPING
& WILDERNESS SURVIVAL

FIRE: THE COMPLETE GUIDE
FOR HOME, HEARTH, CAMPING
& WILDERNESS SURVIVAL

13-Digit ISBN: 978-1-64643-242-4
10-Digit ISBN: 1-64643-242-8

This book may be ordered by mail from the publisher. Please include $5.99 for postage and handling. Please support your local bookseller first!

Books published by Cider Mill Press Book Publishers are available at special discounts for bulk purchases in the United States by corporations, institutions, and other organizations. For more information, please contact the publisher.

Cider Mill Press Book Publishers
"Where good books are ready for press"
PO Box 454
12 Spring Street
Kennebunkport, Maine 04046

Visit us online!
cidermillpress.com

Typography: Arno Pro, Brother 1816

Image credits: Illustrations on pages 9, 13, 28, 42-44, 66-67, 68-69, 71-72, 75, 78-79, 82, 88, 103, 111, 114-115, 118-119, 123-124, and 127 courtesy of Cider Mill Press; photograph on pages 86 courtesy of Cider Mill Press. All other images used under official license from Shutterstock.com.

Printed in China

1 2 3 4 5 6 7 8 9 0
First Edition

4

FIRE

THE COMPLETE GUIDE
FOR HOME, HEARTH, CAMPING
& WILDERNESS SURVIVAL

KY FURNEAUX &
J. SCOTT DONAHUE

CIDER MILL PRESS

BOOK
PUBLISHERS
KENNEBUNKPORT, MAINE

CONTENTS

INTRODUCTION

THE EARLIEST EVIDENCE OF THE FIRST habitually used fires can be found in caves in Africa, Europe, and the Middle East, scattered across the world like telltale shards of burnt bone. The oldest campfire site, dating back to at least one million years ago, was found in South Africa's Wonderwerk Cave, where excavators unearthed cooked animal remains. They also discovered chips of flint, which point to another question: Were our ancestors making arrowheads, or were they trying to create sparks by striking stones?

We may have made our first fires with wood-on-wood friction. It's hard to say when we started making fire with only wood. Building the first form of "friction fire" required the kind of ingenuity only humans have. As we began to build fires, we began thinking about "if-then" outcomes. If we rub hard wood against soft wood, then wood shavings form; if we continue rubbing, then smoke appears; if smoke appears, then coals will form; if the wind is too strong, then coals will go out; if there is a slight breeze, then coals will grow; and so on, went our scientific minds.

Nearing the end of the Lower Paleolithic period some 500,000 years ago, we began to make fire with tools made of wood, string, and stone. With teardrop-shaped hand axes of flint, chert, and agate, we hacked through bone, scraped skin off of meat, made sharper weapons, and chopped wood.

Over time, we developed and improved upon our crude ways to make fire. There was the fire plough that required a great deal of craftsmanship, not to mention patience and practice—and especially tough hands. The hand drill technique similarly required a keen understanding of friction embers. We figured out that a slight breeze can keep a glowing coal going, and recognized patterns in the smoldering dust we made: black, smoking dust makes fire.

Here's an aside: for anyone who has tried drilling for fire, show me the blisters on your palms to prove it. The spindle method is time-consuming, laborious, painful, and seemingly impossible. Only experienced survivalists have perfected this means to make fire—a skill that does wonders for YouTube channel hits. Undoubtedly, an existence spent drilling and plowing wood against wood inspired us to invent more efficient, less infuriating ways to make fire from scratch. So we modified the drill with ropes. We added stone weights. We incorporated bows to do the work for us. This was all Stone Age machinery—the bow drill and pump drill methods—invented to save our poor skin.

Once we had a good fire going, we sent a message to the snarling predators that lurked beyond our encampments: a message of dominance. Fire could keep wolves at bay, except for the curious ones. Fire attracted these wolves to our side. And who could blame them? The irresistible scent of roasted meat, discarded bones and scraps, and the rewarding sensations of a scratch behind the ear and a belly rub came in exchange for loyalty. Wolves that depended on us became our protectors, and we bred those protectors for thousands of years. Fire gave us our proverbial best friends in dogs.

At the dawn of the Bronze Age, stone lost its luster. People 5,000 years ago figured out a way to use fire to mine for copper and bronze. Called "fire-setting," the trick involved placing fire near a rock face, and then dousing the rock with cold water to fracture open the rock to reveal the dazzling metals within. These metals, with the help of fire, could be melted, pounded into shape, sharpened more easily, and traded at a more valuable price than stone. Then bronze and copper tools gave way to iron.

Iron—namely steel, which we manipulated to our design with our mastery of fire—put civilization on a fast track. Steel meant superior knives and axes, more hygienic cookware and utensils, and trusty hammers and nails to build cities that stood plumb and proud for centuries. However, the fundamental advancement of iron was using it to make fire. Rather than crudely chipping away at stones with marcasite or pyrite, we forged and shaped iron to make artificial flints. These looked like bracelets: oblong-shaped, with a side for gripping and another side with a coarse surface that gave off sparks with the brush of a blade. And unlike stone, these could last thousands of strikes without losing their integrity. Iron strikers were such a marvelous invention that we used them until matches could be mass-produced in the mid-nineteenth century.

At some point in our innovative partnership with fire, we learned ways of powering our lives far beyond the kitchen and hearth. During the Industrial Revolution, we burned coal to fuel factories, locomotives, and steam ships.

Around fire's creative and destructive force, we developed culture. Religious rites, dances, sacrifices, and funerals all involved fire. In dancing flames, we found creative answers to explain the mysteries of life. Zoroastrianism, one of the world's oldest religions, treats fire as a purifying medium through which celestial judgment is passed. The Hindu deity Agni is the avatar of fire and sacrifice, and appears in the flames accepting sacrifices from the faithful. And in Exodus, the god of Abraham communicates with Moses in the form of a burning bush. Fire was and continues to be a meeting point between the unknown and us.

1

FIRE
ESSENTIALS

FIRE ESSENTIALS

THE ESSENTIAL ELEMENTS OF MAKING A FLAME are the same, whether you are having a cozy night at home in front of the fireplace, sitting around a campfire with friends and family toasting marshmallows, or needing to start a fire in an unexpected survival scenario. What follows assumes the most extreme circumstances in order to best educate you about how to make and sustain a fire, no matter where you are.

The three things needed to make a flame are oxygen, fuel, and a heat source.

Oxygen is fortunately all around us with the air we breathe, so apart from locating the fire out of the wind and avoiding accidentally smothering the heat source, the preparation for this is minimal.

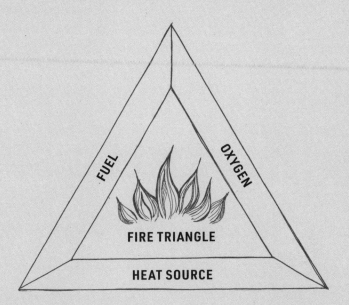

FUEL

OXYGEN

FIRE TRIANGLE

HEAT SOURCE

A **heat source** will take resources or time to make. Even if you have matches or a lighter on you, be aware that these resources are finite, and make sure that you make the most of every match or strike of the lighter.

Fuel is the main thing that you need to prepare before making a heat source. Many people put in a huge effort to make a friction-fire coal, only to have it smolder out while they are frantically searching around for materials to ignite it in. Be aware that most methods of primitive fire making don't finish with you having a flame, they finish with you having a coal, which you then have to nurse into a flame.

FUEL

FIRE FUEL CAN BE broken down into three different types:

- **Tinder**
- **Kindling**
- **Fuelwood**

TINDER

Tinder is any material that takes a minimal amount of heat to make it catch on fire. The key to good tinder is that it must be dry. Look for fine-grain fibers that can fluff up easily when rubbed between your hands. Its purpose is to be a coal or spark extender. This means that it should take the heat from the heat source and be able to either turn it into a flame or make a bigger, hotter coal. Some materials ignite well but burn too quickly to be useful on their own. Dry cattail heads are a good example of this. They work great when combined with other materials but burn out too quickly on their own.

The best way to collect tinder that is ready for your heat source is to make a tinder bundle or bird nest. When a bird makes its nest, it has bigger materials on the outside to keep the structure of the nest and smaller materials on the inside to protect the baby bird. The finest materials should be on the inside, ready to amp up the heat source, and the larger materials should be on the outside, ready to fuel the flame. Good inner materials should almost be the consistency of fluff or dust. Things that work great for this are:

Dry grass; or the inner bark of some trees, rubbed between your hands

Dry cattail head

Bracket fungus (pounded into fine dust)

Dry cattail flower

Palm fibers

Dry dung from grass-eating animals (ground into fine dust)

The outer layer of a tinder bundle should also be mostly fine, dry, combustible material. Dry grass tied into a knot, creating a nest for the smaller materials, works well. You can also use bark, palm fibers, or coconut husk. It's a good idea to experiment in your area to see what works for you. Some dry fibers seem like they might work but don't have the combustible properties to ensure success, so they could lead to you wasting time and energy.

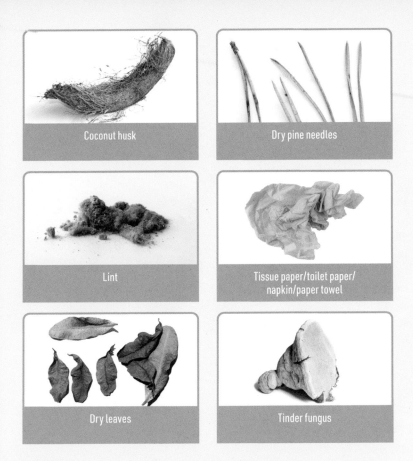

Coconut husk

Dry pine needles

Lint

Tissue paper/toilet paper/
napkin/paper towel

Dry leaves

Tinder fungus

The idea of a tinder bundle is that once you have your coal or heat source, you place it in the center of the bundle and fold over the edges of the bundle, so the coal is touching as much fuel as possible. By firmly (but not wildly) blowing into the bundle, you add enough oxygen for that coal to ignite. This is where the preparation of kindling comes in; without prior preparation, your tinder bundle will quickly burn out, and you will have to begin again.

KINDLING

Kindling is the wood used to extend the flames of the tinder bundle into a useful fire. Think of kindling as being the size of anything from a toothpick to a thumb. Make sure that this wood is also dry, as the tinder bundle flame won't burn long enough or hot enough to dry out wood. Gather a handful of tooth-pick-sized wood, two handfuls of pencil-sized wood, and two handfuls of thumb-sized wood.

Note: dead pine trees tend to have a wealth of flammable wood, made so by the sap and tar pooling at the base of the decaying tree.

FUELWOOD

Fuelwood is what you use to keep your fire going. How well it burns will depend on where you are and the types of wood you have access to. As a general rule, hardwoods burn hotter and longer than softwoods and produce bigger coals.

Assuming you don't have an axe or saw with you, the best way to break up these larger pieces of wood is by smacking them over a rock or bending them between two solid objects (boulders or large tree trunks work). If they are too large to break, you can either place them over the fire and let the fire burn each piece in half for you, or you can feed an end in at a time. This allows you to burn quite large logs that will sustain the fire for a good length of time and also conserves the energy you may burn from trying to break the wood.

As always, you are trying to conserve energy. Do not make a massive fire unless you are trying to signal for help (see page 77 if that's your intent). A small fire will keep you just as warm if it is positioned properly, and it doesn't take much of a flame to boil water.

Try to find dry standing wood or wood that is off the ground, as it will generally be a more solid wood. Any wood that has sat on the ground for a while will tend to be rotten or full of termites and will burn faster than standing wood.

Make sure to collect more fuelwood than you think you will need. You don't want to blunder around in the dark to get more wood, if your fire has gone out and you are freezing. Find a way to store wood that will keep it dry or dry it out. Build a small shelter near the fire that houses your collected wood. And make sure that the wood is off the ground and covered. That way, you're never caught out if it rains.

If you are trying to dry wet wood, place it either around the fire or on a rack over the fire. Just make sure it is not so close that it catches on fire before you want it to.

WOOD TO AVOID

Poison oak leaves

Make sure you avoid the dead wood from poisonous plants, such as poison oak (*Toxicodendron diversilobum* or *T. pubescens*) or, if you find yourself in Australia, the stinging tree (*Dendrocnide moroides*). Smoke from burning poisonous plants can be toxic and cause death or damage to lungs and eyes.

THE BATON METHOD

The baton method of chopping wood requires only a sturdy hunting knife to split through a dense piece of wood.

First, working from the outside in, you lodge the blade into the fuelwood or kindling you wish to split. It may take a few good whacks or a few taps from a blunt object to sink the knife sufficiently into the wood. It helps to knock the bottom of the kindling against a hard surface (e.g., a chopping block). The percussion against the bottom of the log will drive the blade deeper into the wood. Repeat this action until the piece is sufficiently split.

BUILDING THE FIRE

ONCE YOU HAVE ADEQUATE TINDER, kindling, and fuelwood for your fire, it is time to decide how best to make your fire. There are many and varied methods of setting up a fire lay (the structure made with kindling). Some people like to dig a hole to contain the fire, and others like to make a ring of stones. It's a good idea to have some clearly defined fire area so that the fire doesn't sprawl, but that is a personal choice. Just remember that if you line your fire with rocks, you need to make sure that they are not river rocks. Wet rocks or river rocks tend to explode when heated and can cause nasty injuries. To avoid this, bang the rocks together and discard any rocks that sound hollow or are brittle.

The main things to remember are:

- **Try to find a location out of the wind.**

- **Clear the area around where you intend to make your fire.**

- **Make sure the ground isn't damp, and if it is, lay down a branch platform to keep your fire base dry.**

- **Fire burns upward; it will seek its fuel above it, so leave an area at the base of your woodpile to place your tinder bundle in.**

- **Go from smaller wood to larger wood: toothpicks at the bottom of your pile where the tinder bundle will be placed, to thumb-sized wood on top.**

- **Don't pack the wood on too thickly or too thinly; too much wood will smother the flame, and too little won't provide enough fuel, and the flame will burn out.**

THE TEPEE LAY

This is exactly what the name suggests. Prop the toothpick-sized twigs on your cleared ground first, and then layer the outside of them with the pencil-sized twigs, and finally the thumb-sized branches. Make sure not to use all your kindling in the structure, so that you will have some to feed into the fire if you have misjudged how much of each size is needed. Your on-fire tinder bundle is then inserted beneath the toothpick-sized twigs. As the flame burns upward, it will light the toothpicks, which in turn will provide enough sustained heat to light the twigs.

If you have a ready flame such as a match or lighter, you can skip the tinder bundle stage and head straight to making the tepee lay. Just make sure you compensate by filling the space under the toothpick-sized twigs with some smaller, highly flammable material to get burning first.

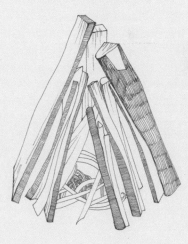

THE LOG CABIN LAY

Again, collect your handfuls of toothpick-, pencil-, and thumb-sized twigs. You will also need two bigger pieces of wood laid out parallel to each other. Scrape out a hole to place the tinder bundle in, and lay the toothpick-sized twigs across the hole, with a handful running one way and a handful running perpendicular (at right angles) to them. The next pencil-sized layer should sit on your two parallel logs, again crisscrossing a layer each, and, finally, the same with the thumb-sized twigs. With this method, you can stack your thicker fuel at the top of the cabin structure early in the process, because it won't collapse in on itself and smother the fire, as can sometimes happen if you put big wood on the tepee structure too soon.

Place the tinder bundle or flame under the toothpick-sized twigs, and you should soon have a fire.

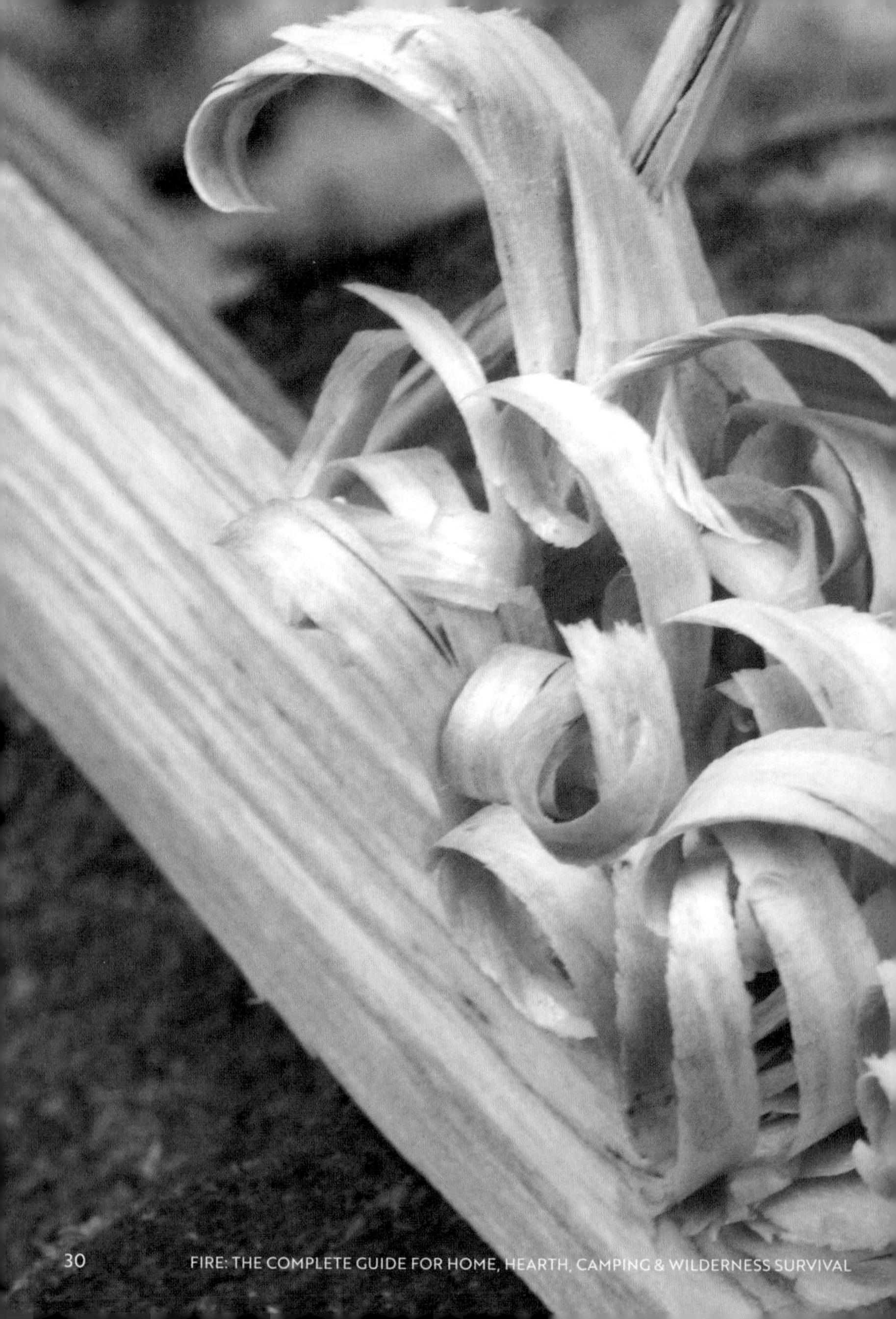

FEATHER STICK

No fire preparation section would be complete without mentioning a feather stick. It is tinder, kindling, and fuel-wood all in one and a popular method of starting fires, especially in adverse weather. If you make one well enough, you can even light it from a spark.

To create a feather stick, choose a straight, dry stick with no knots. Lay your blade flat on the stick and then tilt the angle of the blade slightly toward the wood. Run the blade all the way down the stick, stopping just before the bottom of the stick so that the shaving remains attached to the stick. Turn the stick around and repeat. Keep repeating until you end up with a thin stick with shavings attached. Place this inside your fire lay and add an ignition source.

BASIC TOOLS FOR MAKING AND FUELING FIRE

YOUR TINDER, KINDLING, AND FUELWOOD are ready to be set on fire. But how do you get the flames to rise? Read on.

PLASTIC LIGHTERS

Lightweight, durable, and lasting up to 3,000 lights, these little guys are the most efficient and hands-down-easiest way to make fire from little more than a bundle of dried grass and twigs. They save time, physical effort, and mental energy—three things that must be rationed if you're waiting for a rescue, and worth keeping in mind if you're getting ready to entertain at home. Of course, nature purists and stoic survivalists like *Survivorman* host Les Stroud bristle at the convenience of a lighter, and understandably so.

Part of the joy of "surviving," or the recreational version of it, is overcoming hardship and the challenge of building a fire from what you foraged, not what you can buy at a gas station. But in real, unplanned survival situations, making fire through crude means should be a last-ditch effort, if there are easier ways to make fire available to you. In this situation, take the path of least resistance and use a plastic lighter if you've got it.

ALL-WEATHER MATCHES

If you have objections to a lighter's use of accelerants or to the plastic industry, but you still want reliable means to start a fire in any situation (storms, blizzards, flash floods), then waterproof matches belong in your survival kit and home. Truly, this match is a masterpiece of chemistry. Striking the match on any dry surface produces a slow flare-up that turns into a violent and awesome flare of purple and blue flame, even when lit underwater. Plus, these matches burn for up to fifteen seconds, and it should only take one to light a tinder ball. The secret to making these matches so resilient is this: a wax coating that protects the highly reactive elements—red phosphorus, potassium, or magnesium—on the matchstick. Alternatively, regular kitchen matches will come in handy as well.

FIRE: THE COMPLETE GUIDE FOR HOME, HEARTH, CAMPING & WILDERNESS SURVIVAL

MAGNESIUM BLOCK/FERRO ROD

These handy little gadgets are often called a "flint and steel," which is not accurate to describe them but is a reflection of their past. Historically, people would hit a rock called flint with their steel knife to create a spark to make a fire. As time went by, the ferro rod was invented, combining a mixture of metal alloys into what is called mischmetal. When struck with a steel striker, this mischmetal ignites with a spark that burns hotter and longer than a spark caused by simply striking two natural rocks together, or a rock and a knife.

The problem is that many survivalists and outdoors people put these gadgets in their packs, believing that they have fire sorted, when in reality, they only have a method of getting a spark. The process needs to go one step further to knowing how to get the hottest, most sustained spark and what material will ignite with that spark.

The best way to use a ferro rod is to position the rod so it is facing low and central to your tinder. In the hand holding the striker, brace your knuckles on the ground or your shoe and then sharply pull back the hand with the ferro rod in it. The striker should be at about a 30-degree angle to the rod for best results. If you push the striker toward the bundle, you risk displacing your tinder before the spark reaches it. As with any survival kit, if you choose to have a ferro rod in your bag, make sure you know how to use it and what tinder ignites best with a spark in your area or the area you're visiting.

Most magnesium blocks come with an iron-based striker for your knife to brush against, creating a flurry of sparks. The goal is to connect those sparks with the shavings of magnesium. With a knife, make shavings of magnesium from the block. Shave a pile of magnesium strips onto a ball of tinder until the shavings add up to a "pinch" in terms of measurement.

Then, the fun part: find a comfortable position. Press your knife and striker into the tinder and scrape madly, aiming the sparks at your fresh-shaved metal. The flying sparks will eventually react violently with the magnesium in a tiny but sustained light. Once the magnesium begins to catch fire, carefully close your tinder ball around the shavings. With small movements of your wrist, rock the bundle of burning magnesium until it begins to smoke, and continue until you have a flame.

Ferro Rod

Magnesium Block

HATCHET

Few tools inspire as much reverence and ardor for wood splitting as the hatchet. The hatchet is the Goldilocks of hewing tools: heftier than a knife, too stunted to be an axe—and it fulfills the tasks of both tools, just right. A hatchet can be operated with one hand, and used for chopping on one side and hammering on the other.

Hatchets are more useful in cabin and campground environments than they are in the backcountry. Since they usually weigh in at two to three pounds, a hatchet would weigh you down more than your knife. With that said, the hatchet is the finest and fastest tool to separate kindling out of larger pieces of fuelwood.

To test your blade's sharpness, take a slanted hack at a piece of firewood. If the blade is dull, it'll glance right off the wood. A sharp blade should catch into the side with little effort.

FOLDING POCKETKNIFE

Two mantras apply for starting a great fire: 1) Start small, and 2) You will need a knife. The pocketknife fulfills both. A pocketknife, or any other type of retractable knife ranging from 1 to 4 inches, will do for shaving off splinters, strings, and chips—and other elements that are essential for tinder (see page 15). Pocketknives are also crucial for shaping wood into crude fire-starting tools, if need be.

FIXED-BLADE HUNTING KNIFE

For the same reason we use a steak knife to trim tri-tip, a serrated hunting knife proves its effectiveness by carving into dense sticks and logs. You don't have to have a foot-long knife like Rambo's in *First Blood*; unless you're trying to compensate for something else, a fixed-blade hunting knife doesn't need to be more than 6 inches.

MADE IN U.S.A.

CHOOSING THE BEST FUELWOOD

BEAR IN MIND that the right wood calls for the right situation. Maybe you're looking for wood that crackles, pops, and sparks like well-timed sound effects for your ghost story. Or maybe wood that splits most compliantly with your axe. Maybe you're looking for the most heat per log, or something that burns all night in the hearth. Or maybe you're looking for the smell of citrus, cinnamon, sage, or malt.

British thermal units (BTUs) measure the amount of work needed to raise the temperature of one pound of water to 1°F. To put this in perspective, a kitchen match generates 1 BTU, whereas a cord of firewood ranges between 10 and 24 million BTUs.

ALDER is a straight-grained firewood that splits with ease and burns best when seasoned. Overall, alder is a decent choice for campfires and cabins, for its sweet smell and fast growth.

17.5 million BTUs per cord

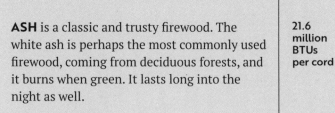

ASH is a classic and trusty firewood. The white ash is perhaps the most commonly used firewood, coming from deciduous forests, and it burns when green. It lasts long into the night as well.

21.6 million BTUs per cord

BEECH grows its silver-gray bark in deciduous forests east of the Mississippi River. Its extremely dense wood takes time to catch fire but burns cleanly without much sparking.

22.7 million BTUs per cord

BIRCH grows in the coldest deciduous forests of the Northern Hemisphere, across Scandinavia, North America, and Siberia. People living in these regions depend on birch's dense fuelwood, water-resistant properties, and flammable and oily bark.

19.5 million BTUs per cord

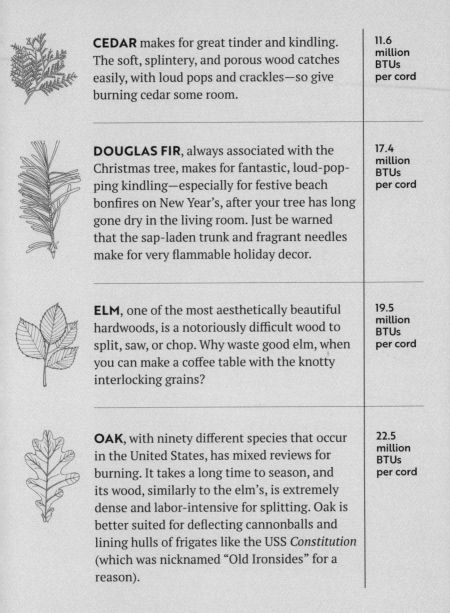

CEDAR makes for great tinder and kindling. The soft, splintery, and porous wood catches easily, with loud pops and crackles—so give burning cedar some room.

11.6 million BTUs per cord

DOUGLAS FIR, always associated with the Christmas tree, makes for fantastic, loud-popping kindling—especially for festive beach bonfires on New Year's, after your tree has long gone dry in the living room. Just be warned that the sap-laden trunk and fragrant needles make for very flammable holiday decor.

17.4 million BTUs per cord

ELM, one of the most aesthetically beautiful hardwoods, is a notoriously difficult wood to split, saw, or chop. Why waste good elm, when you can make a coffee table with the knotty interlocking grains?

19.5 million BTUs per cord

OAK, with ninety different species that occur in the United States, has mixed reviews for burning. It takes a long time to season, and its wood, similarly to the elm's, is extremely dense and labor-intensive for splitting. Oak is better suited for deflecting cannonballs and lining hulls of frigates like the USS *Constitution* (which was nicknamed "Old Ironsides" for a reason).

22.5 million BTUs per cord

PINE works well for campfires, with its snapping, sparking, and scent; however, it can be dangerous to burn indoors. Creosote buildup in chimneys is a huge drawback to burning a citrusy but resin-rich cord of pine. Pine splits into kindling and catches fire with ease, and is best suited for a night of camping in alpine country.

15.3 million BTUs per cord

SUGAR MAPLE, which puts on the pageantry of blazing red leaves during the fall, keeps a good fire long through the winter. Its caramelizing scents make maple an excellent firewood for a woodstove or cabin.

24 million BTUs per cord

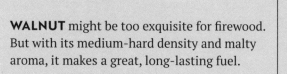

WALNUT might be too exquisite for firewood. But with its medium-hard density and malty aroma, it makes a great, long-lasting fuel.

20 million BTUs per cord

2

SURVIVING
WITH FIRE

SURVIVING WITH FIRE

THERE ARE MANY REASONS why fire is essential to survival. It contributes to all of the other basic needs in some way and adds so much more to your survival on its own. It may make the difference between you surviving and not. In a survival situation, make it a priority to have a fire burning before the sun sets and make sure you have enough wood stockpiled to ensure that the fire is kept burning throughout the night. The fire doesn't need to be a big one. In most cases, simply the smell of the wood burning will be an ample deterrent for potential predators.

Some of the bonuses of having a fire include:

- **Warmth**
- **Protection**
- **Signaling for rescue**
- **Cooking**
- **Psychological benefits**

GO PREPARED

No hiker should ever step out of his or her front door without the commonsense tools needed to survive. You need some way of navigating yourself from your car to your destination and back to your car. You need protection from the sun and the elements, the right insulation, a working headlamp, first-aid supplies, and a tent or tarp. And on a primal level, you need water, food, a knife, and the means to build a fire.

Shoelaces

Paracord

Knife

Lighter

Lens or piece of glass

Granola

Sunscreen

STARTING A FIRE IN A SURVIVAL SITUATION

THE KEY TO GETTING a good fire going is preparation. It doesn't matter if you have fire-lighting methods on you or if you have to improvise—what you do before even making a spark, flame, or coal will be the difference between getting a roaring fire going or wasting valuable resources, energy, and time.

The first thing most people imagine when they think about making a fire in a survival situation is the friction-fire method, or what's better known as rubbing two sticks together. It is a very physically demanding and technical process. Before embarking on the friction method, try an easier method if you have the requisite tools—this will be much simpler and will burn fewer calories.

Do you have a lighter, magnesium block/ferro rod, or matches?

NO

Go to next question.

YES

You'll have little trouble starting a fire! Turn to pages 32 through 36 of Chapter 1: Fire Essentials for tips on how to use them.

Do you have a battery (AA, D, etc.) and some wire?

NO

Go to next question.

YES

BATTERY METHOD
(page 58)

Do you have a lens/magnifying glass and lots of sunlight?

NO

Go to next question.

YES

REFRACTION METHOD
(page 56)

Do you have shoelaces and/or cordage?

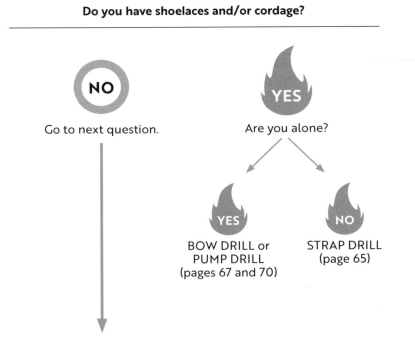

NO

Go to next question.

YES

Are you alone?

YES

BOW DRILL or
PUMP DRILL
(pages 67 and 70)

NO

STRAP DRILL
(page 65)

Can you find dry flint, quartz, or iron pyrite stones nearby?

NO

NO: HAND DRILL or FIRE
PLOUGH (pages 72 and 75)

YES

YES: ROCK-PERCUSSION
METHODS (page 58)

REFRACTION

One of the least strenuous methods of making a fire is to allow the sun to shine through something that will magnify the sun's heat. Of course, everyone thinks of a magnifying glass. If you have one on you, that's a bonus, but there are a few ways of recreating the effects of a magnifying glass in a survival scenario. Human beings have managed to pollute just about everywhere in the world with our garbage, so you can usually manage to find these types of things in quite remote locations. The most obvious is a piece of glass from such items as a broken bottle or a camera lens, but a piece of a plastic bottle will work also:

- **Magnifying glass—your compass usually has a little one incorporated into it**

- **Glasses—if they have a magnifying lens**

- **Clear plastic water bottle—if filled with water, you can use the base to concentrate the sun's rays into a point**

It can also be done with a clear plastic bag full of water and a piece of ice; however, conditions must be ideal for both.

This method will not work at night (for obvious reasons), and the closer the sun gets toward the horizon, the less direct heat there is. This method is best tried in the middle of the day, when the sun is at its peak. Angle the glass so that the sun's light passes through and magnifies onto your pile of tinder. You will see an obvious, yellow patch of light.

If you're using a mirror, reflect the sun's rays until you see a "death ray" appear on your fire nest. Keep your mirror about 6 inches above what you wish to combust. Adjust the space of your glass like a lens, as if to put the sunlight in focus on your target. Too far away, and the light is too dispersed. Too close, and the light is too concentrated.

Get comfortable, because this could take twenty minutes or longer. If you can, find shelter from the sun or cover your back, neck, and head.

WIRING A BATTERY

This method works if you have a flashlight or something that runs on batteries (like a camera). You will also need two pieces of wire; perhaps there is a fence nearby, or you could use the inside of an electrical cord, such as a phone charger.

Attach one wire to the positive end of the battery and one wire to the negative end. When you bring the two wires close together, a spark will jump between them. If you can place your tinder between the wires, you should be able to light it from the spark.

ROCK-PERCUSSION METHODS

All around the world, there are rocks that will create a spark when hit off each other or when hit by a knife with a high carbon content. The spark is generally cooler and faster burning than one produced by a

magnesium block or ferro rod (see pages 35–36), so it is essential to have a good, flammable tinder bundle ready.

Flint

One method is known as the flint-and-steel method. This is because flint is found in most places in the world and dependably produces good sparks when hit with a high-carbon-content metal. **Flint** tends to be a chalky-looking, fine-grained rock that is either light gray or white in color. But most fine-grained rocks that can be broken to have a sharp edge will usually work, if flint isn't readily available.

If you are unsure about how to identify flint, try a variety of rocks lying around to see if one produces a spark. Even if you can't see the spark, sometimes you will smell a distinctive match smell on the rocks after striking. You have to hit the rock quite hard and sharply to get the spark, but once you get the hang of it, it's an easy and reliable fire-lighting method.

Quartz also works with a metal striker, and its white color makes it fairly easy to identify.

Quartz

One stone that will deliver a workable spark when struck off itself is **iron pyrite**. This is less readily found around the world, but there is evidence that some of the most primitive cultures carried with them pieces of this rock specifically to make fire.

Iron pyrite

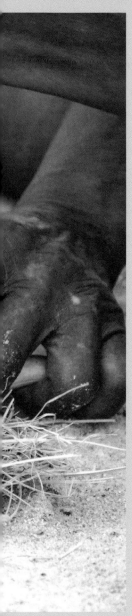

FRICTION FIRES

THERE ARE MANY DIFFERENT forms of friction fire, but they all usually involve rapidly rubbing two pieces of wood together to create enough heat and dust to make a **hot coal**. Learn one or some of these techniques before you take off on your extreme outdoor adventure, because they are very difficult to learn on the fly. However, necessity is the mother of invention, so if you understand the theory behind what works and what doesn't, you may be able to make it work, if your life depends on it.

There are certain woods that work better for friction-fire making than others. Rather than having you learn all the best friction-fire woods in the world, here is a set of properties to determine what will work best for you in your circumstances:

- **Dry**
- **Soft, lightweight wood (but not rotten)**
- **Sourced from faster-growing trees or weeds**
- **Straight—free from bends or knots**

It is better if you choose a slightly softer piece of wood for your **spindle**, with a slightly harder piece of wood for your baseboard, but wood of the same density will work too.

One of the most important things to remember is that both bits of wood must be bone dry. Any dampness in either will probably result in failure. Be aware of how damp the ground you are working on is. Any moisture on the ground will be absorbed into the drier wood and lead to a lack of success as well.

With most of these methods, you will need a **notch** to keep your spindle or drill piece moving in the same place. This will be a hole for the hand drill and bow drill methods and a horizontal notch for the fire plough methods. You will also need a **catchment area** for the **"dust"** you produce.

This dust will be the main indicator of how well your method is working. It needs to be a dark brown, almost black color. If your dust is light in color, you either need to change the pressure of the strokes or the speed of the strokes, usually increasing it rather than decreasing it. This dust is what will combust to form a coal, so make sure it doesn't blow away or fall out of the notch.

Using friction can be a very physically demanding way to get a fire going, so start slowly with your strokes. With the right amount of pressure, you can get heat without rapid movement. As smoke starts to be seen, increase the pace of your strokes and continue for longer than you expected to.

Once you have a smoking coal, take your time and transfer it to your **tinder bundle**. You will have created an excess of dust that will help the coal increase its size over a minute or so, which means you don't have to rush.

If you are unsure if a wood will work, just give it a go. If the wood heats up, changes color, or produces dust or smoke, it is worth putting in a bit of effort with.

Read on to learn about the most common methods of friction-fire making.

STRAP DRILL

This is one of the friction-fire methods that requires the least amount of strength or exertion; children as young as five can master it. This method requires only two additional pieces of equipment compared to the hand drill, but it is a two-person method, so if you are flying solo, then it's not the method for you.

You will need a piece of rope or cordage and a bearing block. If you are wearing laced shoes, then you are in luck. The cord only needs to be as long as a shoelace. The bearing block needs to have a hole or divot in it. If you are using wood, the wood needs to be of a harder wood than the spindle. You can use bones, antlers, rocks, or shells for your bearing block. As long as the spindle can spin freely in the hole, and you can exert some downward pressure without it slipping off the top of the spindle, it should work.

The spindle should be thicker for the strap drill than the bow drill; about the thickness of an adult thumb is a good estimate. One end should be carved to a point, and the other end carved into an arch. The pointy end goes into the bearing block, and the arched end goes onto the baseboard. The baseboard can also be a little thicker—anything up to an inch.

One person will put their foot on the baseboard and exert a downward pressure on the top of the spindle with the bearing block. The other person will wrap the cord around the spindle three or four times, and then pull one side of the cord and then the other, keeping a firm pressure between their hands and allowing the friction of the cord to spin the spindle. As before, carve a divot into the baseboard, burn in the hole, and then cut your notch before putting in a big effort for the coal. Place a leaf or a piece of bark under the notch to catch your dust. The longer and smoother the strokes of the cord, the faster you will get a coal.

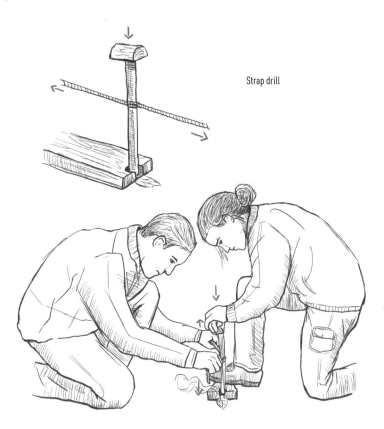

Strap drill

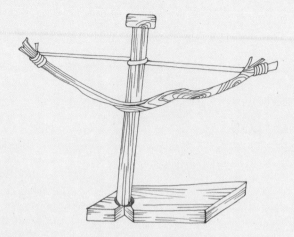

BOW DRILL

This is the next-most-efficient method of friction fire, after the strap drill. The difference is that it can be done with one person, and your piece of cord needs to be stronger than for the strap drill, as it has more pressure on it through the bow. Your shoelace should still work.

You will need a slightly bent stick that you tie the cord to each end of. Some people prefer a small bow, others prefer a bow with a big bend in it, and others like to use a very long bow. A happy medium is a stick about 2 feet long that is almost straight. The reason for this is because it's possible to do nice, long strokes with the bow, but it is manageable and not ungainly. Your bow should be made of a rigid wood, since a flexible wood will lead to your cord slipping on the spindle. The spindle and baseboard can be prepared as for the strap drill.

The cord needs to be fairly firm between the bow ends, because you want it to grip on to the spindle. Twist the spindle so that the cord is wrapped around it once. If the spindle wants to flip out but can be wrapped, that is a perfect tension. The spindle should be on the outside of the cord, with the arched end on the baseboard and the pointed end in the bearing block.

Place your foot on the baseboard and anchor the inside of your left forearm to the side of your shin (assuming you are right-handed). This hand will hold the bearing block firmly in place. With your right arm, move the bow in a long, smooth motion back and forth. If you do this slowly at first, you will conserve energy as you build up heat. Once you see lots of smoke from your dust, put in a final big effort.

PUMP DRILL

The Iroquois invented this handy method of drilling for fire that involves the use of cord. Though pump drills are brilliant Stone Age inventions for creating fire and drilling through stone, they require more energy and engineering; in other words, they aren't recommended for time-sensitive survival situations. One crucial component of the pump drill is a stone weight to fix at the base of your pump drill. This takes the most time and effort to craft. Without a free weight at the base, the pump drill is useless. Built correctly, however, you can get a fire going in under a minute.

You will need:

- **A fixed-blade or hunting knife**
- **A softwood drill stick**
- **A weight, either made from a thin, circular rock or a circular piece of hardwood**
- **A crossbar: a stick of hardwood**
- **A cord or bootlace**
- **A hearth board: a flat, dry, and soft wood**

Take your drill stick, and bore an eyehole near the top. Thread the eye with your cord.

Find a circular rock of about one or two pounds or a circular piece of hardwood, and carefully carve a hole through the center with your hunting knife. Your drill should fit tightly without having the disc slip off, so measure how wide the hole should be in advance. This weight will sit toward the bottom by the pointed end of the drill.

Bore a hole through the center of your crossbar, and bore eyeholes on each end. Fit the drill through the middle hole, and then fasten the ends of the cord through the crossbar's eyeholes. The device should look like a cross.

Twist your drill stick so that the cord is wrapped around. The crossbar should be at the top of your drill.

Set the drill on your hearth board. Pushing down on the crossbar's handles will cause the drill and the weight to spin. The weight's mass and momentum should cause your pump to float upward while the cord recoils back around the drill's shaft. Rewind the crossbar and repeat until the friction creates a fire.

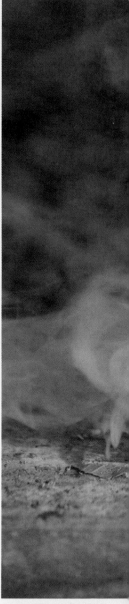

HAND DRILL

This is the simplest friction-fire method, given that it only needs two pieces of wood. It is also one of the hardest, because it requires fairly specific wood types and good upper-body strength to be successful. You will need a straight, thin spindle about a foot and a half long with a half-inch diameter and a base-board about three-quarters of an inch thick. Carve one end of the spindle into an arch. The arched side rests on the baseboard.

Carve a divot into the baseboard to keep the spindle in position, and place your hands flat on either side of the spindle. When you first start learning this technique, you will need to anchor the baseboard in place with your foot. Push your hands together and spin the spindle with a downward pressure to help generate the heat required. If you are creating enough friction, the baseboard will start to smoke, and you will burn a circle into the baseboard. Using a sharp edge, cut a notch into the side of the baseboard that halves the circle, making the circle look like Pac-Man. Place a leaf or a piece of bark under the notch to catch your dust. Repeat the spinning motion until the notch fills up with black dust and begins to smoke. With enough heat and friction, this dust will ignite into a coal.

This action of burning in a hole, cutting a notch, and filling the notch with dust is consistent with both the strap drill and bow drill methods as well.

FIRE PLOUGH

Out of all the friction-fire methods, this one is not highly recommended. For as simple as it looks, it requires a level of angle experimentation that other friction fires lack. It also requires a fair bit of stamina. But if you don't have tools and cordage, it is a good one to try. For materials, it just requires a softer wood baseboard and a harder wood "plough," or you can try it with the same wood. The plough is a piece of straight wood with a flattened, sharpened end of about 30 degrees. The baseboard needs a long, straight groove in it, and it must be on a solid surface or able to be anchored down somehow. It's best to keep both hands on the plough and your arms straight when ploughing. Moving from the waist and pushing forward on the plough means you will have more stamina to keep going longer. Push the plough back and forth in the groove, creating dust at the far side of the groove. As darker dust forms, speed up and give it your all until the dust pile is smoking on its own.

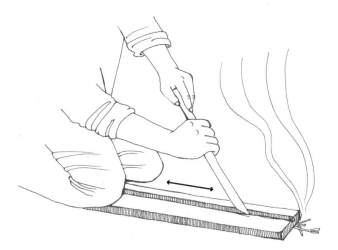

FIRE: THE COMPLETE GUIDE FOR HOME, HEARTH, CAMPING & WILDERNESS SURVIVAL

SIGNAL FIRES

LET'S SAY YOU'VE GOTTEN LOST in the wilderness. First, you should stop and take a few deep breaths. If you can retrace your steps, then do this until you're sure again. But if the sureness doesn't come, and you find yourself confounded by the mesmerizing thickets of pines and disquieting solitude, then you have a decision to make: Should I stay or should I go?

Unless you find better cellular reception on a hilltop, or a natural calamity occurs, opting to stay where you are is your best bet.

One of the first things to do when thrown into an extreme survival situation is to construct—by any means—a fire to signal for help.

Construct your signal fire on a hilltop, or in a clearing in the woods or on the beach. If you are lost in the middle of the day, use materials that will smoke heavily: leaves, green wood, grass— the damper, the better.

Distress signals are universally a series of three. Building a group of three signal fires will not only create a larger smoke cloud, but will also effectively communicate your emergency. If you have enough time, energy, or space, create an SOS or HELP out of branches.

Group of three
signal fires

FIRE IN THE DESERT

SOMEHOW, YOU ARE LEFT TO SURVIVE in the hot, arid, soul-baring emptiness of the Mojave or Sonoran. But thank your lucky stars that you came prepared with a wide-brimmed hat, sunglasses, light-colored shirt and pants that minimize sweat loss, and sunblock with a high Ultraviolet Protection Factor (UPF). You drank your fill of water before your hike and refilled the bottle again and again before leaving the parking lot (rather than rationing your water like a fool). And you informed someone—a friend or family member—where you would be hiking, and for how long.

Now what?

If you're stranded in the desert without matches or a lighter, you may need the power of the sun to build a signal fire. Lucky for you, dry sage and dead saguaro are excellent kindling to get a modest fire going. The challenge, of course, is to harness the heat of that energy-sapping ball of fire in the sky and aim the rays at a bundle of desert-dry tinder. Look back at pages 56 through 57 for how to use lenses to start fires.

FIRE IN SNOW AND ICE

YOU'RE POST-HOLING through alpine country, lost in a thicket of snow-laden conifers, and the sun is getting lower. If you don't have a tent and a sleeping bag, your chances of surviving the night without a fire are low. Fire is simply a must to keep your clothing dry, your spirits up, and your body from slipping into hypothermia.

The trick to getting a fire going in the dead cold is to make it happen in one go. The work of building a fire will bring temporary warmth to your body, but the evaporation of sweat, mixed with heat convection from touching cold objects, will suck the life out of you the longer you take to build your fire.

Pick a place for your fire that isn't directly under branches. It's so frustrating to finally have your fire going, only to have a drooping, snow-covered branch dump its weight onto your only hope of surviving! Find a clearing that will accommodate a fire close to the opening of your lean-to, snow cave, or other improvised shelter.

Once you've found your site, tramp down the snowpack with your boots in a 4-foot-wide circle. Then, start digging with either a shovel or your gloved hands until you hit ice. Take your knife or hatchet, and start hacking away at the ice until you've hit dirt.

On the south side of a pine tree—a low-hanging source of fuel exposed to the sun—you'll find sticks, bark, and dry branches to use for your fire. First, find materials to make a dry bed for your tinder. Lay these materials out crisscrossed to create a dry platform above the wet ground. Then, with your tinder and kindling close by (and out of the way from snow), construct your tepee or log cabin lay, with a small opening to receive your flaming ball of tinder.

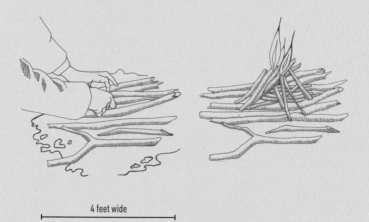

4 feet wide

SUSTAINING YOUR SURVIVAL FIRE

IN A SURVIVAL SITUATION, it's always best to keep a fire burning constantly. This way, you don't have to worry about taking the time to light one every night, and you have a signal ready at any time if a plane flies overhead or a ship passes by your island. You should have a pile of wood that you keep specifically for signaling, so that you're not unprepared if your rescuers come close by. Green boughs work best for creating thick smoke to help attract attention.

In order to sustain a fire without having to constantly attend to it, you will need to set your fire in such a way that it burns slowly but has access to fuel as needed.

This largely depends on what type of wood you use, but can also depend on how you set your fire. Hardwood burns hotter and for longer, and softwood burns colder and quickly. But there are certain types of wood that hold heat and smolder. Mallee roots in Australia are a good example of this. They will rarely ignite fully but will glow and maintain a coal that you can blow to a flame by adding kindling when you need it.

It's good to be observant of the woods you are able to access and use on the fire and what properties they have (see page 42). Choose the ones that burn hot and bright to bring water to a boil quickly, and the ones that smolder to keep the fire going during the day. Punk wood, wood that has gotten soft and rotten and then dried out, is fantastic for creating a smoky fire, if you want to smoke meats or hides, or keep insects away.

Placing a large hardwood log into a fire will keep it burning for a while, and you can also place logs in a star formation and feed them inward when necessary.

Building a solid crosshatch structure and lighting a small fire on top of that will allow the fire to slowly burn downward through the wood without it burning upward quickly.

If your fire has gone out while you were away from it, try digging down into the ash and coals with some small, flammable materials handy. Chances are there is enough heat left in the hot coals below the surface to ignite your tinder.

MOVING FIRE FROM ONE PLACE TO ANOTHER

MANY ANCIENT CIVILIZATIONS valued fire so much that it was one person's specific job to take care of it when the tribes traveled from place to place. It is way easier to blow a fire alight from a coal than exert the effort required to start a fire from scratch. Transporting fire was done in a variety of ways, but the theory was the same: allow a coal to have just enough oxygen and fuel that it stays lit, without it being smothered from a lack or burning itself out from consuming it all.

The design was fairly similar to a tinder bundle, with small materials around a hot coal, wrapped tightly to prevent too much oxygen from getting in. A large animal horn works well, but you can also use some kind of flexible bark tied together with a strip of inner bark.

When traveling with coals, it is a good idea to check on them every now and then to see if they need more fuel or oxygen. It's also a good idea to carry a dry tinder bundle with you, so you can fuel the coal immediately to flame when you get to your next campsite.

REFLECTIVE FIRES

USUALLY, THE BEST THING TO DO in a survival situation is to stay put and wait for rescuers to come to you. If you do have to be on the move, you can use a reflective fire to keep safe and warm at night. This is less labor-intensive than a shelter and can be much warmer.

The key is to find a flat wall surface at least 3 feet high. Lie between this and a low-burning, body-length fire that you've built a windbreak on the other side of. This is not a good option if you think it may rain (definitely build or seek a shelter if this is the case), and you must also make sure you have enough wood to last the night, as a 3:00 a.m. wood collection run is never a good thing.

A reflector wall can also be built if you have a permanent shelter. Simply build a windbreak on the opposite side of your fire. Although most heat rises, some heat will bounce off the wall and into your shelter, and it will also cut back on the heat that gets pushed away by the wind.

If you choose to locate your fire inside your shelter, due to extreme cold or an abundance of biting insects, make sure that your roof is high enough that it doesn't catch fire and that you maintain a low, cooler fire.

FIRE RULES TO REMEMBER

- Clear an area around your fire
- Don't light a fire you can't control
- Don't light a fire at the base of a standing tree
- Always make sure your fire is fully out before permanently leaving an area

3

FIRE AT HOME & IN THE BACKYARD

FIRE: THE COMPLETE GUIDE FOR HOME, HEARTH, CAMPING & WILDERNESS SURVIVAL

FIRE AT HOME & IN THE BACKYARD

NOW YOU KNOW HOW to build a fire with limited resources. This is invaluable knowledge, but hopefully you never need to put it into practice out of necessity. So now let's focus on having fun by the fire—safely, of course.

We told our first stories sitting around a fire. Poets recited epics centering around super-human athletes, cunning thieves, or tricksters shaped like the animals familiar to the land. All of these mythical characters somehow bestowed upon humankind a strange, wondrous light. The moment we beheld this light, we instantly separated ourselves from the animal world. We held a light that warmed our bare skin in the winter, cooked our food, warded off predators, and captured our imagination. Our mastery of this light proved our control over nature—or at least gave us the illusion of it. A roaring fire in the fireplace or backyard firepit never fails to bring back those ancient instincts.

THE FIREPLACE

CARING FOR A FIRE in the home means having the necessary tools within arm's reach. These items allow the tender to shift logs, agitate coals, sweep ash, and dispose of the excess remains:

- **Fire poker**
- **Tongs**
- **Shovel**
- **Brush**

Make sure your damper is open. It looks like a thin metal plate with a hinge connected to the chimney. Use the lever to open the damper to keep the flow of smoke traveling upward through the chimney, rather than filling the living room with smoke. The correct way of using a damper is to open it completely as you're getting your fire started. Then, when the fire is off and roaring, lower the damper a few notches until the lack of airflow weakens the fire and smoke begins to collect. Open the damper notch by notch, until the smoking ceases.

Stuff the bottom of the grate with newspaper, cardboard, or pages from an old phone book. Magazines or glossy paper don't burn well and only add smoke and toxic fumes to the process.

Set starter wood in the center of the grate. Start small, and use splintery pieces of kindling to make a foundation to the little log cabin you're about to construct. Lay three pieces of kindling down, spaced apart by an inch. Then add another layer of kindling perpendicularly to make a second layer.

Add larger pieces of kindling. Continue building your log cabin using three to four pieces of kindling for each layer. Remember to leave room for ventilation.

Get the fire going with a single match. With a sturdy log cabin, ready to burn on top of your fire grate, set a match on multiple edges of the newspaper underneath. The flames should move across the tinder paper with ease. The flames will travel upward from the newspaper, catch splinters in the kindling, and spread upward.

Adjust the fire with tongs or a poker. Fires don't always begin in perfect health. Smoking furiously or dwindling early sends a message to the fire tender that adjustments need to be made. Use these wrought-iron tools to move your kindling with slight adjustments so as not to ruin the structure. A dwindling fire that hasn't caught the kindling means you must add more tinder; plumes of smoke mean you must create more space between the kindling.

WOOD-BURNING STOVES

WHILE FIREPLACES ARE AESTHETICALLY pleasing, wood-burning stoves have a few more advantages. First invented in the mid-sixteenth century, these cast-iron contraptions are space heaters and cooktops all in one. Old models of stoves are definitely contributors to poor air quality, especially for launching soot and carbon dioxide into the atmosphere. However, newer EPA-approved wood-burning stoves have improved so much in design that they make less of an environmental impact than fireplaces, which pump out eight times more CO_2 gases than EPA-approved stoves.

SHOVELING ASH

Clear out the remains of the previous fire by scooping out the excess ash from the bottom of the fire grate to create airflow. Before disposing of the remains in your green waste bin, first make sure the ash is cool to the touch and that there are no glowing coals, and perhaps even dispose of the ash in a metal can just in case.

HOME FIRE SAFETY

PUTTING OUT A FIRE is never as simple as throwing a bucket of water onto a flame. In fact, water can worsen an out-of-control fire, depending on its fuel source. Different classes of fires require different extinguishing agents.

FLAMMABLE LIQUIDS

Petroleum gasoline, ethanol, paint, and other flammable liquids can be put out by an opposing chemical chain reaction. DON'T use water to put out these fires. Instead, use a dry chemical extinguisher. This multipurpose fire extinguisher does the job on most fires, so it's good to have one in the kitchen or garage. These extinguishers stop the exothermic reaction with an agent that blocks the exchange between oxygen and fuel.

GREASE FIRES

The kitchen is a common place for spontaneous, uncontrolled fires to jump from a pan or oven. If it's a grease fire, use baking soda. DON'T splash water onto a grease fire; it's the worst thing you could do. Water separates from oil immediately, which causes scalding grease to splatter.

Here are some steps to put out a grease fire:

- **Turn off the burner. There is the potential for burning oil to splatter and contact your skin, so be advised not to move the pan.**
- **If the fire is small, smother it with baking soda. The chemical properties of baking soda ($NaHCO_3$) allow for the powder to release carbon dioxide when in contact with a flame. Baking soda is also a product in fire extinguishers.**
- **If the fire is larger (e.g., coming from a deep fryer), cover the pan with a metal lid to smother the flames.**

FIRE: THE COMPLETE GUIDE FOR HOME, HEARTH, CAMPING & WILDERNESS SURVIVAL

BUILD YOUR OWN BACKYARD FIREPIT

BEFORE YOU BUILD A FIREPIT, it's important to familiarize yourself with the local laws in regard to the property (see pages 104–105 for some examples).

- Avoid having your firepit under tree branches. Find an open space in your yard, where you can look up every once in a while from the flames to see open sky.

- A firepit ought to be 3 feet in diameter and a foot deep. To build your own firepit, all you need to do is dig these dimensions and line the rim with bricks or pavers.

- Cover the bottom of the pit with bricks or pavers, creating a dry hearth for your fire. This also creates a barrier between your wood and the damp soil beneath the bricks.

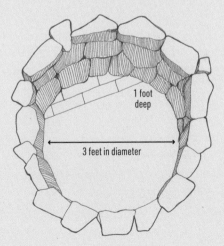

1 foot deep

3 feet in diameter

CHECK YOUR MUNICIPAL CODE

HERE ARE SOME SAMPLE EXCERPTS of municipal code language dealing with backyard firepits. Wherever you live, be sure to check your local municipal fire regulations before building and starting your first fire outside.

A: PORTLAND, OREGON

- Recreational fires [are] defined as: burning clean, dry, cord-type firewood as in a standard campfire-type setting. When burning a fire of this type, you must build the fire in a pit or pan prepared for this purpose.

- The fire must not be larger than a standard campfire, less than 3 feet in diameter, with [a] pile less than 2 feet in height.

- A responsible person shall be in attendance at all times and have approved fire-extinguishing equipment close at hand.

B: COLUMBUS, OHIO

- No less than 10 feet from any combustible structure (house, fence, shed, etc.); apartment buildings may require 25 feet.

- Recommend a water source and/or fire extinguisher located near and readily available for immediate use.

- Firepits cannot be used during "Air Quality Alert" days.

C: BALTIMORE, MARYLAND

- Small recreational firepits no larger than 3 feet in diameter are allowed; these can be purchased or self-constructed.

- There must be one person 18 years of age or older in attendance until the fire is out and there are no smoldering embers.

- Fires and other open-flame cooking devices must be at least 15 feet from multifamily dwellings, apartments, and condos.

THE ART OF SPLITTING WOOD

CHOPPING WOOD is a lot like the exquisite craft of needlepoint: solitary, intricate, and even therapeutic. Best of all, you get to handle a sharp object. But like any other refined craft, proper wood chopping requires a great deal of precision and accuracy. An accurate wood-chopping technique requires you to home in on a near-perfect bisection of wood, whereas precise wood chopping depends on your consistency and repetition in the pursuit of a more perfectly parsed piece of wood. So please, please, please be sure to keep your eyes open.

PERSONAL PROTECTIVE EQUIPMENT (PPE)

Gloves. Some work gloves are dipped in latex rubber; while this aids in keeping a good grip with a saw, they aren't recommended for chopping or hammering in a wedge. For those splitting chores, you need gloves that will keep your hands from getting cold, chapped, or blistered, while allowing free movement from the axe's shoulder to its throat on the downswing.

Glasses. Have you ever seen a lumberjack cry? If so, it's for no other reason than a piece of wood lodging itself in an eyelid and triggering a tear. Otherwise, a safe woodworker avoids this painful situation by wearing protective eyewear.

Heavy boots. If you need any reason to wear heavy or even steel-toed boots while standing at the chopping block, think of the baseball commentator's mantra: "Swing and a miss." Boots are simply common sense when dealing with heavy chunks of wood and a sharp object.

THE AXE: YOUR INDISPENSABLE WOOD-SPLITTING TOOL

LIKE CHOOSING THE right baseball bat, pick the axe according to your own height and strength. For beginners, a five-pound axe head is sufficient. Also, consider the length of the handle (also knows as the haft). Long hafts give the user an advantage of greater force on the chop; however, shorter axes allow for more accuracy and control.

For the express purpose of splitting wood, find a single-bit axe with a concave cheek. This particular shape ensures a quick and easy bisection of the wood, while preventing the head from sticking. Hafts are usually made of hickory or ash. Hickory is a mainstay for axes, with its compressed grain and shock resistance. Ash, similarly, is good enough for major league baseball bats. And while wood inevitably wears down, or develops chips and cracks, hafts are easy to replace. When it comes to handles, varnish sucks. A varnished handle chips more easily after use, is hard on your hands, and is more slippery than an untreated handle.

THE ANATOMY OF AN AXE

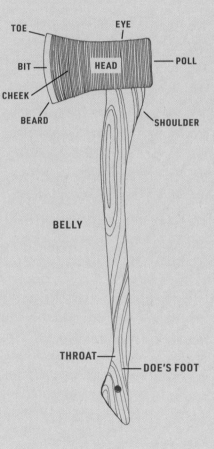

TOE

EYE

BIT

HEAD

POLL

CHEEK

BEARD

SHOULDER

BELLY

THROAT

DOE'S FOOT

AXE SAFETY

- A glancing blow to the shin is an all-too-common injury. It's better to aggressively follow the rules and play it safe than end up in the hospital.

- Clear the area around you. There shouldn't be any roots, rocks, trees, or branches within an axe-length (the length of your axe and your arm) of you and your logs.

- Create an "axe yard" by measuring two axe-lengths around, and make a boundary to show others that there are sharp edges nearby.

- Make a chopping block by sawing a log so that it is about 2 feet high, and stand it upright.

- Make it easy on yourself and aim for cracks in the log first. Avoid knots, and turn a log over so the knots are on the bottom, allowing for the bit to hit clean wood first. If you get tired, rest.

- When you're not cutting wood with your axe, muzzle it with its sheath. If one isn't around, avoid that lumber-jack temptation of throwing it over your shoulder. Instead, point the cutting edge down and away from you as you walk.

A RUSTY AXE IS AN EASY FIX

Using steel wool or coarse-grit sand-paper that contains aluminum oxide or silicon carbide, rub the axe head in a circular, buffing motion. When the rust is sufficiently removed, use a rag and metal polish for a new-blade sheen. To keep your tools from rusting again, apply linseed or even motor oil.

GET YOUR LUMBERJACK ON

The action of lifting an axe targets the upper back, shoulder, and bicep muscles, while the downswing requires your abdominal muscles to engage and curl. And as with weight lifting, your gains in fitness depend on the proper technique. Once you understand the correct motion in all of its parts, you can turn it into one fluid and effective motion.

An hour at the chopping block burns 400 to 500 calories—or more, if you're doing it in the dead of winter.

1. Grasp the axe's shoulder with your dominant hand, and place your other hand low on the grip. The dominant hand will slide, while your other hand will provide crucial leverage on the downswing. The axe blade should be facing downward, and the shaft should be parallel to the ground.

2. Raise the axe over your head. As the axe reaches the apex directly above your head, slide your dominant hand down the shaft. The dominant hand will slide down to meet your other hand. Don't forget legwork. Your legs should go into a quarter-squat, while your feet should be a little more than shoulder-width apart and square to the wood you are cutting.

3. Swing the axe downward forcefully onto the awaiting piece of wood. For extra velocity of the tool, snap your wrists along with the axe. Your hands should create a fulcrum-lever motion that will give you that extra thunk!

SHARPENING AN AXE

No wonder we "keep our nose to the grindstone" when faced with tedious work; sharpening an axe takes repetitive strokes. There's little doubt that pedal grindstones—used as far back as the fifteenth century—can hone an axe to perfection. But for DIY purposes, all you will need are these:

- **Bastard file**
- **Vice**
- **Circular whetstone (also called a "puck")**
- **Linseed oil**
- **Leather gloves**

First, stick the axe head securely in the vice, with the edge pointed outward. With a file, slide lightly along the edge as if to gently blunt the blade. This action removes chips and nicks along the blade edge. Keep going until the rough edge becomes smoothed out under the file. This will create burrs—shiny flecks of exposed metal—on each side of the blade.

Next, grab the file with both hands end to end. At an angle of roughly 25 to 30 degrees, slide the file downward into the blade—and only in this direction—all along the edge. The leather gloves should protect your fingers in this process. Remove the new burrs you made with the initial filing, and settle in, because this process should take hours of honing.

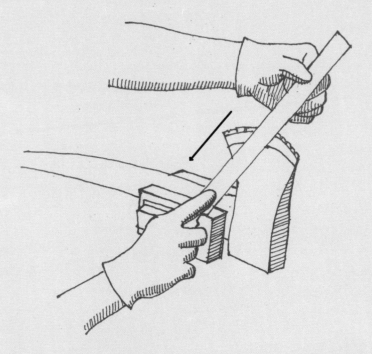

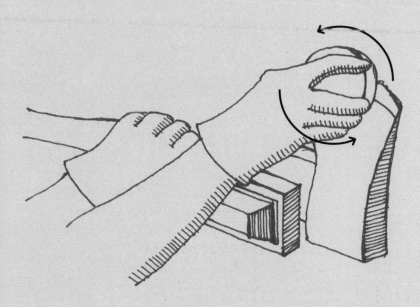

The finishing touch on your blade involves a circular whetstone and a little bit of linseed oil. The oil, when applied conservatively to the whetstone, floats metal particles off of the axe. The motion used with the whetstone is similar to "wax on" (you'll be ready for the All Valley Karate Tournament in no time). Circular movements concentrated close to the arc of the blade should create a "fanned" effect on the bit. The mark should look like an arc about 3 inches from the blade on a "flat-ground" axe, or a ½-inch chisel for your average hardware store blade.

STACKING FIREWOOD

THE PROCESS OF STACKING and keeping seasoned wood dry at home involves little more than a shed. However, for those without a shed or a rack, effective stacking techniques are simple. It's important to keep ventilation in mind when putting each piece of wood in place. Firewood, when kept outside in the elements, should be uncovered and spaced a couple of inches apart. For sturdy piles, each log when stacked against the other should correspond in shape.

FIRE: THE COMPLETE GUIDE FOR HOME, HEARTH, CAMPING & WILDERNESS SURVIVAL

TOWERS

Somewhat like setting up a game of Jenga, building a tower stack is ideal for fuelwood that is short in length (especially helpful for making solid ends to your pile). Stack three pieces side by side, but with a couple of inches of breathing room. Then, stack another layer of three perpendicularly, and continue this pattern until it reaches chest level. Continue building these towers until you get a pile of wood that resembles a cord (8 feet long, 4 feet high, 3 feet deep). You can cover the top with a tarp, but don't completely cover it. This lets the wood dry out and keeps it from collecting condensation under the plastic.

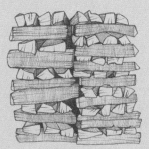

CORD WALL

A little more straightforward than building a tower, a cord wall is exactly what the name suggests. Find a place alongside your house that gets plenty of sunlight, and preferably where the wood can be laid out from east to west. Then, begin setting your wood perpendicularly to the wall. The advantage of this stacking method is the efficient use of space, combined with the ease of removing the wood when it's time for a fire. One cord equals 128 cubic feet of wood.

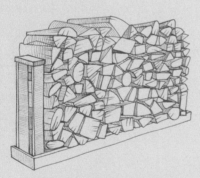

SHAKER STYLE

This method of creating a circular woodpile takes a little more calculation. Your wood should be equal in height and width, so start with creating a circle with your firewood equal to the height you think the end result will be. Start by forming a ring with your chopped wood. Add layer upon layer, raising the walls as if each piece of wood were a brick for a humble home. Fill the center of the ring with uneven pieces of wood—these will prop up the "roof" of your Shaker-style pile.

Once you have finished fortifying the walls of your silo-shaped stack of wood, you can top off the pile and shape it like a cone. Use a tarp to cover only the top, and use extra pieces of wood to weigh the tarp down.

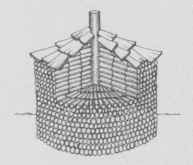

4

CAMPING
& COOKING
WITH FIRE

CAMPING & COOKING WITH FIRE

WE STEP INTO THE PAST when we camp around a fire. When we converse and eat meals with a fire nearby, we reenact a nightly human ritual performed since the beginning of our species. Camping—taking temporary residence among the sequoias, in an arena of mountains, or on a high desert plain—brings us closer to our self-reliant selves.

WHY YOU ONLY USE WOOD YOU BUY FROM THE CAMP STORE

ALL PARKS HAVE A STRICT CREDO when it comes to firewood: "Buy it where you burn it." Bringing foreign wood to burn in a carefully preserved habitat is not only against park regulations, but also it can lead to an invasion of pests and diseases, subsequently causing the deaths of hundreds of millions of trees. Invasive species include the emerald ash borer, bark beetle, Asian long-horned beetle, and gypsy moth.

The invasion happens when their shelters inside the firewood get too hot for their liking. So they move out of the firewood and make their new homes in nearby trees. These pests, along with alpine drought and an increasingly warming climate, leave a wake of dead wood and standing tinder just waiting to flare up in a wildfire.

CAMPGROUND CAMPFIRE RINGS: THERE FOR A REASON

RESPECT THE FIRE RING. Most campsites in national and state parks will have designated spots for campers to light fires. The presence of a campfire ring rules out any other location for building a fire. And if there is no fire ring at your campsite, it's safe to assume that campfires are probably prohibited.

Park rangers and forestry officials chose these rings at campsites for a reason. Usually constructed with an iron band, fire rings are built away from trees and underground roots.

CABIN CAMPING

Cabins evoke the humble beginnings of American selfreliance. Lincoln's childhood home, Thoreau's cabin at Walden Pond, and the secluded log house you found on Airbnb share a common bond: a fireplace or stove to stir the walls with radiating heat. Even a run-down hunting shed in the middle of nowhere can feel like a mansion with the simple splendor of a fire going. For tips on working the fireplace or woodstove, see Chapter 3.

CAMPFIRE COOKING

OUTDOOR COOKING using cast-iron cookware is rustic and satisfying. It's also a bit of an art, and not quite as simple as just having the right tools. There are several things you need to factor in before tackling it for the first time. Once you've mastered the basics, though, you'll be off and running and won't ever need to look back.

Anytime you're considering cooking outdoors, the absolute first thing to do is to make sure the surroundings are perfectly safe. If you'll be cooking in a public area like a park or campground, you need to seek out and check all posted signs and make sure fires are allowed, and, if so, that it hasn't been designated a "high fire risk" day. If your area doesn't issue fire warnings, use your best judgment.

Check the area carefully to see if there are any major hazards. There should be no dry material within 10 feet of where you'll be building the fire. The area around your firepit or campfire should be cleared of any debris or otherwise flammable materials.

If you're digging your own firepit, see page 103.

If you're using an existing pit or grill, make sure there is no debris or trash that needs to be removed. Other users may not have been as conscientious or courteous as you.

You are now ready to build a fire. Revisit Chapter 1 for the instructions on setting up your tinder, kindling, and fuelwood.

Are you going to cook on a **grate** or use a **tripod**? A grate is best if you will be using a pan or Dutch oven. A tripod is the only choice if you're using a round-bottomed cauldron or a Dutch oven with a hanging loop handle (that part is essential). You also have the option of cooking directly on the fire, which is best done with three-legged cauldrons or a skillet. Lastly, you can bury a Dutch oven directly into the embers.

A GRATE WITH A SKILLET OR DUTCH OVEN

To set up a grate for cooking, make sure it is as level as possible, and that it will not fall over. It should be sturdy enough to hold all of the cookware you plan on placing on it. Set the grate over the fire using **gloved hands** and **tongs**. To use a skillet, place the skillet on a grate while wearing a **heavy mitt**.

A DUTCH OVEN WITH A TRIPOD

A tripod has three legs and a sturdy chain that hangs from the center. Set it up prior to building your fire. Make sure it is very stable and that it can handle the weight of a full Dutch oven.

Using a Dutch oven suspended from a tripod is the ideal method for making campfire baked beans, chili, stews, and soups. You will need at least one-third of the vessel to hold liquid (stock, broth, wine, water, etc.), and then you're free to fill the rest with your selections of vegetables, protein, beans, hearty grains, and seasonings. As your meal cooks, make sure to stir periodically.

PLANNING FOR THE PERFECT CAMPFIRE MEAL

The best meals cooked over a campfire are the ones that have only a few ingredients, all of which come to life when kissed by fire. To make the most of your experience, try to do all of the prep work for your meal before you head out. Have all of the ingredients, tools, and equipment you will need ready to go.

No matter what you're cooking, you'll need a small amount of fat in a hot pan, the product—a sausage, a freshly caught and cleaned fish, or even some nice vegetables—seasoning (salt at the very least), and heat. This also works for Dutch ovens. For baking, try simple stir-and-pour cakes to start.

ROSEMARY & BLACK PEPPER SCONES

Yield: 4 to 6 Servings · Active Time: 30 Minutes · Total Time: 50 Minutes

While these are a bit savory for an early breakfast, they are a hit for brunch, when they can very nicely complement a simple omelet.

3 cups all-purpose flour, plus more for dusting

2½ teaspoons baking powder

½ teaspoon baking soda

1 teaspoon salt

1½ sticks of unsalted butter, chilled, cut into pieces, plus more to grease

1 tablespoon dried rosemary

1 tablespoon freshly ground black pepper

1 cup whole milk or half-and-half

1. Position a grate over the fire using gloved hands and tongs. Make sure the grate is as secure and level as possible.

2. In a large bowl, whisk together the flour, baking powder, baking soda, and salt. Add the butter pieces and mix with a fork so that the dough is somewhat crumbly.

3. Stir in the rosemary, black pepper, and milk or half-and-half, being careful not to overmix.

4. With flour on your hands, transfer the dough to a lightly floured surface. Form the dough into a circle about ½ inch thick. With a long knife, cut the dough into 12 wedges.

5. Butter a cast-iron Dutch oven, then place the scone wedges in a circle, leaving some space between the pieces. When the coals are glowing, cover and bake for 20 to 25 minutes, or until the scones are golden, turning the Dutch oven every few minutes to avoid burn spots.

CHEDDAR & JALAPEÑO SCONES

Yield: 4 to 6 Servings · Active Time: 30 Minutes · Total Time: 50 Minutes

The spiciness of jalapeño livens up any meal. For an added kick of flavor, split the cooked scones in half and put a spoonful of sour cream and some sliced avocado in the middle.

2 cups all-purpose flour, plus more for dusting

1 teaspoon baking powder

½ teaspoon salt

1 teaspoon freshly ground black pepper

4 tablespoons unsalted butter, chilled, cut into pieces, plus more to grease

¾ cup grated sharp cheddar cheese

½ cup sliced or chopped jalapeño pepper

½ cup whole milk

1 egg, beaten with a little milk

1. Position a grate over the fire, using gloved hands and tongs. Make sure the grate is as secure and level as possible.

2. In a large bowl, whisk together the flour, baking powder, salt, and black pepper. Add the butter pieces and mix with a fork so that the dough is somewhat crumbly.

3. Stir in the cheese, jalapeño, and milk, being careful not to overmix.

4. With flour on your hands, transfer the dough to a lightly floured surface. Form the dough into a circle about ½ inch thick. With a long knife, cut the dough into 12 wedges.

5. Butter a cast-iron Dutch oven and then place the wedges in a circle, leaving some space between the pieces.

6. Brush the wedges with the beaten egg. When the coals are glowing, cover and bake for 20 to 25 minutes, or until the scones are golden, turning the Dutch oven every few minutes to prevent burn spots.

Variation: Ramp up the heat by substituting pepper jack cheese for the cheddar, or substitute a serrano pepper for the jalapeño.

CLASSIC CORNBREAD

Yield: 4 to 6 Servings · Active Time: 1 Hour · Total Time: 3 to 4 Hours

---

If you're going to make bread in cast iron, you have to make cornbread. In fact, many restaurants now serve cornbread right in a cast-iron pan.

---

4 cups finely ground yellow cornmeal

¾ cup sugar

1 tablespoon salt

4 cups boiling water

1 cup all-purpose flour

1 tablespoon unsalted butter, melted, plus 1 teaspoon

2 eggs, lightly beaten

2 teaspoons baking powder

1 teaspoon baking soda

1 cup whole milk

1. In a large bowl, combine the cornmeal, sugar, salt, and boiling water. Stir to combine and let sit for several hours in a cool, dark place. Stir occasionally while the batter is resting.

2. When ready to make, position a grate over the fire, using gloved hands and tongs. Make sure the grate is as secure and level as possible.

3. Add the flour, the 1 tablespoon of melted butter, eggs, baking powder, baking soda, and milk to the batter. Stir to thoroughly combine.

4. When the coals are glowing, heat a cast-iron Dutch oven and melt the teaspoon of butter in it. Add the batter.

5. Cook for 15 minutes, turning the Dutch oven every few minutes to avoid burn spots. Move the Dutch oven farther from the center of the fire and cook for another 40 minutes, or until the cornbread is golden brown on top and set in the center.

BISCUITS

Yield: 4 to 6 Servings · Active Time: 20 Minutes · Total Time: 40 Minutes

For fluffy buttermilk biscuits, you need to work with a very hot Dutch oven. The golden crust on the bottom is as much of a delight as the airy, warm dough.

2 cups all-purpose flour, plus more for dusting

1 teaspoon sugar

1 teaspoon salt

1 tablespoon baking powder

1 stick of unsalted butter, cut into pieces

½ cup buttermilk, plus 2 tablespoons

Variations: Biscuits can be served with savory or sweet additions. You can make miniature ham sandwiches by splitting the biscuits, putting some mayonnaise and grainy mustard on them, and putting in a slice of fresh-baked ham. You can fill them with scrambled eggs and bacon bits. You can slather them with butter and your favorite jam or honey. Or just eat them as is.

1. Position a grate over the fire, using gloved hands and tongs. Make sure the grate is as secure and level as possible.

2. In a large bowl, combine the flour, sugar, salt, and baking powder.

3. Using a fork or pastry knife, blend in 6 tablespoons of the butter to form a crumbly dough. Form a well in the middle and add ½ cup of the buttermilk. Stir to combine and form a stiff dough. Using your fingers works best. If it seems too dry, add 1 tablespoon more of the buttermilk, going to 2 tablespoons if necessary.

4. When the coals are glowing, put the remaining butter in a cast-iron Dutch oven.

5. Put the dough on a lightly floured surface and press out to a thickness of about 1 inch. Cut out biscuits, using an inverted water glass. Place the biscuits in the Dutch oven and bake for about 10 minutes, turning the Dutch oven every few minutes to avoid burn spots. When the biscuits are golden on the bottom, remove from heat and serve.

SIMPLE SKILLET SALMON

Yield: 4 to 6 Servings · Active Time: 20 Minutes · Total Time: 30 Minutes

Start with super-fresh fish, and keep it simple—butter, lemon, salt, and pepper—and you can create a succulent dish that is ready in no time.

3-4 lbs. skin-on salmon fillets

2 tablespoons unsalted butter, cut into pieces and softened

1 lemon, halved

Salt and pepper, to taste

1 tablespoon olive oil

1. Position a grate over the fire using gloved hands and tongs. Make sure the grate is as secure and level as possible.

2. Rinse the fillets with cold water to ensure that any scales or bones are removed and pat them dry with paper towels. Rub the butter on both sides of the fillets, squeeze lemon over them, and season with salt and pepper.

3. When the coals are glowing, add the olive oil to a 12-inch cast-iron skillet. Add the fillets, flesh side down. Cook on one side for about 3 minutes, then flip them and cook for 2 minutes on the other side. Remove the skillet from heat and let the fish rest in it for a minute before serving. The skin should peel right off.

CLASSIC BURGERS

Yield: 3 to 4 Burgers · Active Time: 30 Minutes · Total Time: 30 Minutes

A burger hot off the grill is a delicious thing. It's a staple of American dining. But if you want the best burger ever, you won't produce it on the grill. You'll make it in a cast-iron skillet. Why? Because the fat in the meat creates its own sauce, helping to brown and flavor the meat as it cooks.

1 lb. ground beef

Vegetable oil, for the skillet

Salt and pepper, to taste

Hamburger buns, for serving

Slices of cheese (optional), for serving

Lettuce, tomato, onion (optional), for serving

Ketchup, mustard, pickles, mayonnaise (optional), for serving

1. Position a grate over the fire using gloved hands and tongs. Make sure the grate is as secure and level as possible.

2. When it's time to make the burgers, brush a 12-inch cast-iron skillet with a thin sheen of oil. Don't overhandle the meat, simply take a handful of it (about 3 oz.) and form into a patty. Make 3 or 4, depending on how many will fit in the skillet.

3. Put the patties in the skillet and don't touch them. Let them start to cook. Sprinkle some salt and pepper over them. Let them cook on one side for about 3 minutes.

4. When you flip the burgers, if you want cheese on one or all of them, put it on now.

5. Leave the burgers to cook on this side for 3 or 4 minutes. Scoop the burgers off the skillet with the spatula, slide each one onto a bun, top with whatever you like, and enjoy.

GREEN BEANS WITH BACON

Yield: 4 Servings · Active Time: 10 Minutes · Total Time: 15 Minutes

As contemporary culture continually asserts, you can never go wrong with bacon. Smoky, salty, and buttery, the balance of flavors it possesses is unmatched. Here it is charged with lifting green beans to transcendent heights, a task it handles beautifully.

6 slices of uncured bacon

2 cups trimmed green beans

Salt and pepper, to taste

1. Position a grate over the fire using gloved hands and tongs. Make sure the grate is as secure and level as possible.

2. When the coals are glowing, heat a 12-inch cast-iron skillet for 5 minutes, until it is hot. Add the bacon and cook until it is browned, about 6 minutes. Transfer to a paper towel–lined plate to drain. When cool enough to handle, crumble into bite-sized pieces.

3. Remove all but 2 tablespoons of the bacon drippings from the skillet. Add the green beans and sauté, while tossing to coat, for about 4 minutes. The green beans should be bright green and just tender. Remove from the skillet and season with salt and pepper.

4. Sprinkle the crumbled bacon on top and serve.

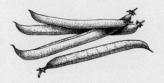

CRISPY & TENDER ASPARAGUS

Yield: 4 Servings · Active Time: 20 Minutes · Total Time: 30 Minutes

When making asparagus in a skillet, the outside gets crisp while the inside becomes tender. The thinner the asparagus, the faster the stalks will cook, so if you are working with super-fresh, thin stalks, you may need to reduce the cooking times in the recipe.

3 tablespoons olive oil

1 bunch of thin asparagus, woody ends removed

1 garlic clove, minced

½ teaspoon salt

½ teaspoon freshly ground black pepper

Lemon wedges, for serving

1. Position a grate over the fire using gloved hands and tongs. Make sure the grate is as secure and level as possible.

2. When the coals are glowing, place a 12-inch cast-iron skillet over the grate. When hot, add the oil and let that get hot. Add the asparagus. Using tongs, keep turning them so they cook evenly in the oil. Cook the asparagus until they are bright green and hot on the outside but tender on the inside.

3. Add the garlic, salt, and pepper, and shake the pan to distribute evenly. Cook for another 2 minutes. Transfer to a serving platter and serve with lemon wedges.

BEFORE YOU LEAVE CAMP: A CHECKLIST

WHEN YOU'RE DONE with your firepit, you need to make sure there's no danger of it reigniting, and check that you haven't littered or polluted the area. Here are the seven steps you should follow to extinguish a campfire, based on the USDA Forest Service guidelines:

1. Drown the campfire with water.

2. Mix the ashes and any partially burned sticks and embers in with the soil.

3. Stir the ashes, embers, partially burned sticks, and soil with a small shovel, making sure everything is wet.

4. Using a bare hand, feel everything, making sure it is completely cool. If not, add more water.

5. When you think you are done, wait a few minutes and check again that everything is cool and wet.

6. Inspect the area and make sure there are no sparks or embers. It only takes one to start a fire.

7. "If it is too hot to touch, it is too hot to leave."

Visit lnt.org (Leave No Trace) and smokeybear.com for more information about parkland fire safety.

ABOUT CIDER MILL PRESS BOOK PUBLISHERS

Good ideas ripen with time. From seed to harvest, Cider Mill Press brings fine reading, information, and entertainment together between the covers of its creatively crafted books. Our Cider Mill bears fruit twice a year, publishing a new crop of titles each spring and fall.

"Where Good Books Are Ready for Press"

Visit us online at
cidermillpress.com

or write to us at
PO Box 454
12 Spring St.
Kennebunkport, Maine 04046

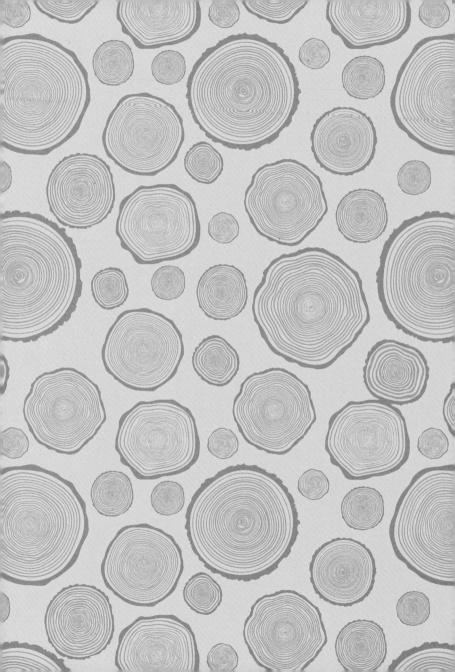